LEICEST
COUNTRY RECIPES

COMPILED BY
PIPPA GOMAR

RAVETTE BOOKS

Published by Ravette Books Limited
3 Glenside Estate, Star Road
Partridge Green, Horsham,
Sussex RH13 8RA
(0403) 710392

Production: Oval Projects Ltd.
Cover design: Jim Wire
Typesetting: Repro-type
Printing & binding: Nørhaven A/S

All recipes are given in Imperial and Metric
weights and measures. Where measurements
are given in 'cups', these are American cups,
holding 8 fluid ounces.

The recipes contained in this book are traditional
and many have been compiled from archival sources.
Every effort has been made to ensure that the recipes
are correct.

RECIPES

SOUPS and BEGINNINGS

FISH

GAME

MEAT

PUDDINGS

CAKES and BREAD

LEICESTERSHIRE

Leicestershire is an unspoilt county at the heart of the shires. The western part of the county was, in the 12th century, covered by Charnwood Forest, though little is left now, and the eastern part of the county is gently rolling pastureland, excellent for the grazing of cattle and sheep.

It is a county well-known for its fox hunting, which probably arose as a substitute for the stag hunting that was popular in the great Charnwood Forest but fell into decline over the centuries as the forest declined. When the sport became popular again in the 19th century, small woods were planted between the open fields to provide habitats for foxes to live and breed. Culinary dishes such as Salmon Kedgeree, Hunting Nuts, Huntsman's Cake, Spiced Beef and Quorn Roll became part of the hunting tradition.

Melton Mowbray is considered to be the centre of the hunting country and is the meeting place for the three most famous county hunts — Quorn, Cottesmore and Belvoir. The market town is also widely known or its pork pies — pies which orginated to satisfy the appetites of the hunters as far back as the 14th century and are still 'raised', or moulded here, in the traditional way.

The area around Melton Mowbray is also famous for its cheese making. Cream cheese making was an established cottage industry in the 17th and 18th centuries.

Leicestershire's rich pastures feed herds of dairy cows, which in turn produce creamy milk which is particularly good for the production of two famous cheeses — Red Leicester and Stilton. The whey, a by-product of cheese-making, makes an excellent foodstuff for pigs which in turn provide pork for the pork pies.

Red Leicester cheese was originally made on small farms when it was shaped like a flat barrel and weighed 45 lbs (20 kg). The deep orange colour was made with a dye formed from an extract of carrots and is now made using a dye called annatto.

Stilton cheese is also made in Leicestershire, although there are several stories about its origin and how it came to have its name. It seems to have been named after the village of Stilton in Huntingdonshire where it acquired its fame, though there is little doubt that it was originally produced in Leicestershire. The cheese is cylindrical in shape and may be white or creamy-yellow with greeny-blue veins. It is made from full-cream milk and forms its own crust. One of the jobs of the Leicester town crier used to be to read a list of penalties against producers of under-weight or poor quality cheese. The crier is even today paid a Stilton cheese and a bottle of port at Christmas time. The tradition of eating Stilton with port seems to have come from the process of dripping wine or beer over the cheese during its production.

The green pastureland of Leicestershire supports both cattle and sheep. Daniel Defoe, travelling through the county in the 18th century, commented on the livestock: 'The sheep bred in this county are, without comparison, the largest, and bear not only the greatest weight of flesh on their bones, but also the greatest fleece of wool on their backs of any sheep of England.'

Public houses named 'The Golden Fleece' and 'The Shoulder of Mutton' show that this animal was important to the economy of the county. Robert Bakewell, a farmer who was born in Leicestershire, became famous for his scientific breeding of livestock. He produced the 'New Leicester' sheep which were transported to London for sale because of the quality and quantity of meat. The county town of Leicester boasts one of the largest and oldest markets in the country. It has been held on the same site for at least 500 years and was famous even in the Middle Ages for the quality of its meat.

Leicestershire was also known by the curious name of

'bean-belly Leicestershire' because of its extensive crops of beans which were considered good enough for men to eat rather than merely an animal feed. Beans, therefore, formed part of the staple diet, especially in poverty-stricken times. There is a saying which goes: 'Shake a Leicestershire yeoman by the collar and you will hear the beans rattle in his belly'.

The old county of Rutland, once known as the smallest county in England, has been part of Leicestershire since the county boundary changes of recent times. It is a rural area renowned for centuries for its production of barley. The people of the area are very proud of their famous Ruddles beer, brewed from the barley. The area also boasts the largest man-made lake in Britain. Rutland Water is visited by people from far and wide and is especially good for the fishing of brown and rainbow trout.

The traditional dishes and the wide variety of food eaten in Leicestershire, reflect the well-rounded agricultural state of the county. It is an area rich in traditions and customs, many of which are still preserved.

'Meet me at the sunset
Down in the green glen,
Where we've often met
By hawthorn trees and foxes' den,
Meet me in the green glen.'

John Clare

STILTON AND CELERY SOUP

Serves 4

1 head of celery
2 onions
2 oz (50 g) butter
1 oz (25 g) flour
2 pints (1.15 litres/ 5 cups) stock
12 oz (350 g) tomatoes
4 oz (100 g) Stilton cheese
A little salt and pepper
8 crayfish tails
A little salt and pepper

Thinly slice the celery and the onions.

Gently cook in the butter for 10 minutes.

Skin, chop and add the tomatoes.

Cook for another 5 minutes.

Add the flour and continue cooking for a few minutes.

Gradually add the stock.

Bring to the boil and simmer, covered, for 30 minutes.

Mash the Stilton cheese with a little of the hot soup to make a creamy paste.

Remove the soup from the heat and add the mashed cheese.

Stir well to allow the cheese to melt.

Liquidize or rub through a wire mesh sieve.

Serve hot.

CARROT SOUP

Serves 6

1 lb (450 g) carrots
2 onions
1 small turnip
1 head of celery
2 oz (50 g) butter
1 oz (25 g) flour
2½ pints (1.4 litres/ 6¼ cups) mutton or beef broth
A large slice of ham
Salt and pepper
A little cayenne pepper

Chop the carrots, onions, turnip and celery.

Gently fry the vegetables in the butter for about 10 minutes.

Sprinkle on the flour and cook for a few more minutes.

Gradually add the mutton or beef broth.

Chop the ham and add to the soup.

Cover and simmer for 30 minutes or until the vegetables are completely tender.

Season with a little salt and pepper.

Liquidize the soup or rub through a wire mesh sieve.

Serve with fried bread and a pinch of cayenne pepper sprinkled on each serving.

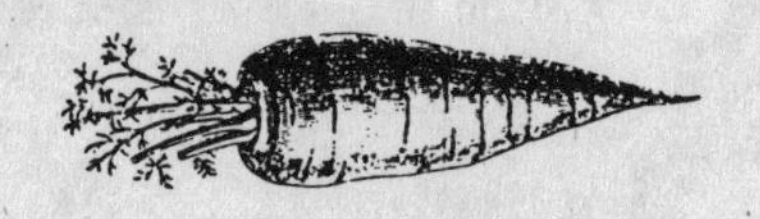

SAXE COBURG

Serves 6

This is simply a Brussels sprout soup. It was called Saxe Coburg by the Victorians, who loved to give dishes lavish names. Leicestershire is one of the main producers of Brussels sprouts.

12 oz (350 g) Brussels sprouts
1 onion
2 oz (50 g) bacon
2 oz (50 g) butter
1 oz (25 g) flour
1 teaspoon caster sugar
A pinch of mace
A pinch of black pepper
2 pints (1.15 litres/ 5 cups) ham stock
½ pint (300 ml/ 1¼ cups) milk
¼ pint (150 ml/ ⅔ cup) dry white wine
A little salt

Wash and chop the Brussels sprouts.

Chop the onion and bacon.

Put the Brussels sprouts, onion and bacon in a saucepan with the butter.

Cook gently for 15 to 20 minutes.

Sprinkle on the flour and stir.

Cook for a further 5 minutes.

Add the sugar, mace, black pepper, stock, wine and milk.

Bring to the boil and simmer for about 15 minutes until the Brussels sprouts are completely soft.

Liquidize the soup or rub through a wire mesh sieve.

Season with a little salt if necessary and serve with croûtons.

GAME SOUP

Serves 6

This thick soup is associated with hunting.

2 lbs (1 kg) venison with some bone *or*
1 game bird and 1 rabbit
1 onions
2 carrots
1 small turnip
1 head of celery
4 oz (100 g) mushrooms
A few sprigs of rosemary and thyme
A large pinch of ground ginger
A large pinch of freshly ground pepper
A large pinch of salt
4 pints (2.25 litres/ 10 cups) stock
¼ pint (150 ml/ ⅔ cup) sherry
1 oz (25 g) butter
A few sprigs of parsley

Remove all the meat from the venison, game bird or rabbit.

Cut the meat into small pieces.

Put the bones into a large saucepan.

Chop the onion, carrots, turnips, celery and mushrooms.

Put the vegetables into the saucepan with the bones.

Add the stock and season with salt, pepper, rosemary, thyme and ginger.

Bring to the boil and simmer, covered, for 3 hours.

Strain the stock and leave to cool.

Remove the fat from the stock when cold.

Just over an hour before the soup is needed, fry the meat in the butter for a few minutes.

Add the meat to the stock.

Pour in the sherry.

Bring to the boil and simmer for 1 hour.

Garnish with parsley and serve with bread.

ANCHOVY TOAST

Serves 6

This savoury was traditionally eaten after a hunt.

1 tin of anchovies
2 oz (50 g) butter
1 tablespoon lemon juice
6 slices of bread

Mash the anchovies and the butter together until well combined.

Add the lemon juice.

Toast the bread and cut each piece into 3 strips.

Spread the anchovy butter on to the strips.

Place under the grill for a few minutes.

Serve immediately.

BUTTER BEAN SOUP

Serves 8

There is a village in Leicestershire called Barton-on-the-Beans. It serves as a reminder that beans formed part of the staple food of the country folk.

1 lb (450 g) dried butter beans
4 pints (2.25 litres/ 10 cups) water
2 onions
2 carrots
1 bouquet garni
1 pint (600 ml/ 2½ cups) milk
A little salt and freshly ground black pepper

Soak the beans overnight.

Drain, rinse and boil in the water for 1 hour.

Chop the onions and carrots finely.

Put the chopped vegetables, bouquet garni and a little salt and pepper into the pan with the beans.

Simmer for a further hour.

Add the milk.

Remove the bouquet garni and liquidize the soup or rub through a wire mesh sieve.

Serve hot with brown bread and butter.

POTTED STILTON

Serves 6-8

4 oz (100 g) butter
1 lb (450 g) Stilton cheese
A little powdered mace
A pinch of salt
4 tablespoons port
Clarified butter

Beat the butter and cheese together.

Season with the mace and salt.

Add the port and beat well to combine.

Press into small ramekins or one larger dish.

Cover the mixture completely with clarified butter to seal.

Chill well before serving.

FRIED TROUT

Serves 4

4 trout
A little salt and pepper
1 oz (25 g) flour
3 oz (75 g) butter
8 oz (225 g) blanched split almonds
2 tablespoons of lemon juice

Gut and clean the fish inside and out.

Season the flour with salt and pepper.

Roll each fish in the seasoned flour.

Melt the butter in a large frying pan.

Fry the trout in the butter allowing about 4 to 5 minutes on each side or until the fish is done.

Remove the fish from the pan and keep warm.

Brown the almonds in the remaining butter in the pan.

Squeeze the lemon juice into the pan and stir well.

Pour the flavoured butter and almonds over the fish and serve immediately.

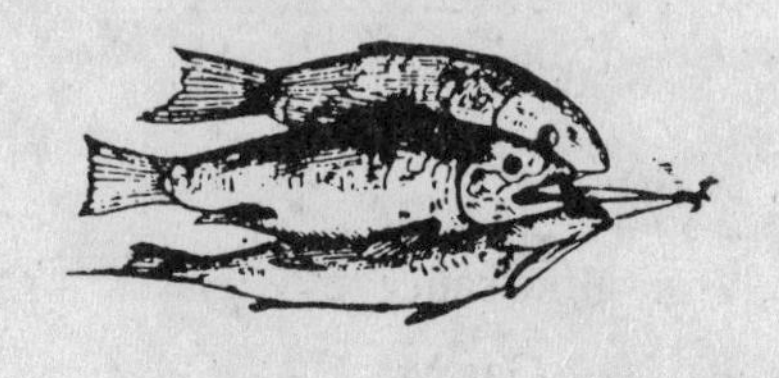

BAKED STUFFED TROUT

Serves 4

4 trout
4 oz (100 g) breadcrumbs
4 oz (100 g) butter
Grated rind and juice of 1 lemon
A little salt and pepper
1 egg yolk
1 oz (25 g) flour
½ pint (300 ml/ 1¼ cups) milk
A few sprigs of fresh parsley to garnish

Clean and gut the trout and remove the fins and gills.

Melt half the butter in a pan and add the breadcrumbs, lemon rind, salt and pepper.

Remove from the heat and beat in the egg yolk to form a firm stuffing.

Stuff the cavity of the trout with the stuffing.

Place the stuffed fish in a greased, ovenproof dish.

Dot with a little more butter and bake for 30 minutes.

Meanwhile melt the remaining butter and add the flour to make a roux.

Cook for a few minutes and gradually add the milk.

Stir until the sauce has thickened.

Pour the sauce into the ovenproof dish with the fish and stir until the fish juices and sauce are combined.

Add the lemon juice and return to the oven for a few minutes.

Serve the dish with the sauce and garnish with parsley.

Oven: 350°F/180°C Gas Mark 4

SALMON KEDGEREE

Serves 6

This was served in the 18th century for breakfast before a day's hunting. It would probably have been followed with kidneys, bacon and slices of cold beef.

The salmon would have been left over from the previous day. Today it makes a good lunch or supper dish.

1 lb (450 g) uncooked long grain rice
12 oz (350 g) cooked salmon
3 oz (75 g) butter
3 hard-boiled eggs
1 tablespoon chopped parsley
A large pinch of salt

Cook the rice. (The cooking time and amount of water will depend on whether brown or white rice is used.)

Remove any skin or bones from the salmon.

Melt the butter in a large saucepan.

Add the cooked rice and the salmon.

Chop the hard-boiled eggs and add to the kedgeree.

Mix well.

Add the parsley and salt.

Turn into an ovenproof dish.

Cover and bake for 5 minutes.

Oven: 350°F/180°C Gas Mark 4

PARTRIDGE WITH CABBAGE

Serves 4

Many old recipes for game birds include cabbage.

4 partridges
4 shallots
Salt and pepper
8 rashers of bacon
4 carrots
4 onions
1 white cabbage
1¾ pints (1 litre/ 4½ cups) stock
¼ pint (150 ml/ ⅔ cup) sherry
A pinch of dried thyme

Prepare the partridges, reserving the neck and giblets to make the stock.

Put a shallot inside each bird.

Season inside the cavity with salt and pepper and rub the outside skin with salt and pepper.

Truss each bird and tie 2 bacon rashers over the breast of each.

Slice the carrots and onions and place in the bottom of a large casserole dish.

Place the partridges on top of the vegetables.

Bake for 30 minutes at the higher temperature, turning often.

Par-boil the cabbage whole.

Cut the cabbage into 8 pieces and pack around the partridges in the casserole dish.

Pour the stock and sherry over and sprinkle with a little thyme.

Cover and cook for 2-3 hours at the lower temperature.

Oven: 375°F/190°C Gas Mark 5
Reduce to: 300°F/150°C Gas Mark 2

VENISON IN BEER

Serves 6

Venison usually featured at the feasts of nobles, who gained much pleasure from hunting stags. Hunting deer had almost died out in England by the 18th century and was replaced by fox hunting. Marinades were frequently used at that time to break down the tougher meat fibres.

3 lbs (1.5 kg) stewing venison cut into cubes
1 pint (600 ml/ 2½ cups) beer or ale
1½ lbs (675 g) parsnips
3 oz (75 g) butter
1 oz (25 g) flour
A little salt and pepper
1 tablespoon treacle
1 oz (25 g) sugar
2 tablespoons redcurrant jelly

Marinate the venison for 2 hours in ½ pint (300 ml/ 1¼ cups) of the beer or ale.

Slice the parsnips and gently fry in 1 oz (25 g) butter.

Transfer the parsnips to a large casserole dish.

Drain the meat but reserve the beer.

Season the flour with salt and pepper.

Toss the meat in the seasoned flour until well covered.

Fry the meat in the remaining butter to seal.

Transfer the meat to the casserole.

Add the remaining flour to the butter and juices in the pan and cook for a few minutes.

Gradually add the marinade, the remaining beer, the treacle and the sugar.

Cook gently until slightly thickened, then pour into the casserole dish.

Cover and cook for 2 hours.

Remove from the oven and stir in the redcurrant jelly.

Serve hot.

Oven: 300°F/150°C Gas Mark 2

RABBIT AND MUSHROOM PUDDING

Serves 4

1 rabbit, prepared and jointed
1 lb (450 g) suet pastry
1 large onion
8 oz (225 g) mushrooms
8 oz (225 g) bacon rashers
A little salt and pepper
A pinch of dried sage
¼ pint (150 ml/ ⅔ cup) stock

Line a 2 pint (1.15 litres/ 5 cups) pudding basin with ¾ of the suet pastry.

Slice the onion.

Chop the mushrooms and bacon rashers.

Layer the rabbit joints, onion, mushrooms and bacon in the basin.

Season each layer with salt, pepper and sage.

Pour in stock.

Cover with the remaining pastry, moistening the edges to seal.

Cover the pudding with buttered greaseproof paper and then foil. Tie down with string.

Put in a large pan filled with enough water to come half way up the sides of the pudding basin.

Steam for 2 hours.

Serve with boiled potatoes and a rich brown gravy.

SMOTHERED RABBIT

Serves 4

This is a very old dish.

1 rabbit, skinned and jointed
½ pint (300 ml/ 1¼ cups) cider
½ pint (300 ml/ 1¼ cups) stock
2 lbs (1 kg) onions
¾ pint (450 ml/ 2 cups) milk and water mixed
4 oz (100 g) butter
1 oz (25 g) flour
A pinch of salt and pepper
½ pint (300 ml/ 1¼ cups) double cream
1 teaspoon lemon juice
A little nutmeg

Put the rabbit joints, cider and stock in a large saucepan.

Bring to the boil and simmer, covered, for 1½-2 hours until the rabbit is tender.

Slice the onions and put into a saucepan.

Add the milk and water and simmer until the onion is completely tender.

Drain off the stock and keep for soup.

Stir in the butter and flour.

Heat gently for a few minutes.

Whip the cream until thick and stir into the onions.

Add the salt, pepper and lemon juice and sprinkle with grated nutmeg.

Remove the meat from the rabbit bones and place on a serving dish.

Smother the rabbit with the onion sauce and serve immediately with boiled potatoes.

HARE PIE

Serves 4

This pie is best eaten cold. It is still made in the pretty village of Hallerton on Easter Monday. Hare-Pie Scrambling is a ritual that has taken place in the village on that day every year since 1770. The rector of the parish provides two hare pies for the event. The pies are cut into pieces and put into a sack and the village men scramble for a piece of the pie on the nearby Hare Pie Hill.

For the filling:
4 joints of hare
1 tablespoon chopped fresh mixed herbs
A little salt and pepper
¼ pint (150 ml/ ⅔ cup) cider
1 pint (600 ml/ 2½ cups) stock made from the bones, head and neck of the hare

For the pastry:
12 oz (350 g) flour
A pinch of salt
3 oz (75 g) lard
3 fl oz (4½ tablespoons) milk and water mixed
1 egg

To make the filling:

Chop or mince the hare meat, reserving the bones to make the stock.

Add the chopped herbs, salt and pepper.

Soak in the cider overnight.

To make the pastry:

Sift the flour and salt together.

Heat the lard, milk and water gently, until the lard has melted.

Gradually mix the liquid into the flour.

Knead the dough until smooth.

Roll out ⅔ of the pastry dough and line a pie dish.

Leave to rest for 30 minutes.

Fill the pastry case with the drained meat.

Roll out the remaining pastry dough and cover the filling, moistening the edges to seal.

Make a hole in the lid of the pie.

Brush with beaten egg to glaze.

Bake at the higher temperature for 20 minutes. Reduce the temperature and continue baking for 1 hour.

Cover the pastry with foil if it looks as though it will burn.

Leave the pie to cool.

Heat the jellied stock and pour into the pie through the hole.

Leave the pie until completely cold.

Oven: 400°F/200°C Gas Mark 6
Reduce to: 350°F/180°C Gas Mark 4

BEEF IN A BLANKET

Serves 4

This dish is also known as Beefy Toad and resembles the well known dish Toad-in-the-Hole.

For the meatballs:
12 oz (350 g) minced beef
4 oz (100 g) breadcrumbs
1 onion
1 tablespoon Worcestershire sauce
A large pinch of mixed herbs
A little salt and pepper
1 egg

For the batter:
4 oz (100 g) flour
A pinch of salt
1 egg, separated
½ pint (300 ml/ 1¼ cups) milk

To make the meatballs:

Mix the mince and the breadcrumbs together.

Grate the onion and add to the mixture.

Add the Worcestershire sauce, herbs, salt and pepper.

Beat the egg and add, mixing well.

Make the mixture into 8 small balls.

Arrange these in a greased ovenproof dish or roasting tin.

To make the batter:

Sift the flour and salt.

Add the egg yolk.

Gradually add the milk, beating all the time.

Whisk the egg white until stiff, and fold into the batter.

Pour the batter over the meatballs.

Bake for about 45 minutes or until well risen and browned.

Oven: 400°F/200°C Gas Mark 6

BAKED SUET DUMPLING

Serves 4

This traditionally accompanies roast meat, and is cooked in the oven at the same time.

6 oz (175 g) self-raising flour
5 oz (150 g) shredded suet
A pinch of salt
A little milk to mix

Sift the flour and mix in the suet.

Add a pinch of salt.

Pour in enough milk to make a soft dough.

Knead the dough on a floured board and shape into a circle about 1 inch (2.5 cm) thick.

Place on a greased baking tray and score the top of the dough with a cross.

Brush with milk and bake for about 30 minutes or until well risen and browned.

Oven: 350°F/180°C Gas Mark 4

HUNTING BEEF

Serves 10

In Victorian times on the day of the hunt the hunters, who would be riding all day, required a substantial breakfast. A joint of beef was pickled and cooked to serve at breakfast on the day of the hunt. The remainder was used as filling for sandwiches taken in the hunters' pockets.

3 lbs (1.5 kg) joint of beef (silverside or brisket is best)
6 oz (175 g) salt
A pinch of salt petre
1 oz (25 g) soft brown sugar
A pinch of ground mace
2 cloves
2 bay leaves
¼ pint (150 ml/ ⅔ cup) ale

Mix the salt, salt petre, sugar, mace and cloves in a bowl.

Crumble the bay leaves and add to the ingredients in the bowl.

Rub the mixture into the beef.

Leave in a cool place for 10 days.

Rub the mixture into the beef every day. The mixture will become liquified.

Rinse the meat and drain.

Put the meat in a large saucepan with the ale.

Add enough water to cover the meat completely.

Bring to the boil and simmer, covered, for 2 hours or until tender.

Serve either hot with boiled potatoes and vegetable or leave to get cold.

STEAK AND KIDNEY PIE

Serves 6

8 oz (225 g) puff pastry
1½ lbs (675 g) rump steak
12 oz (350 g) ox kidney
1 oz (25 g) flour
A little salt and pepper
1 onion
2 oz (50 g) butter
8 oz (225 g) mushrooms, sliced
1 pint (600 ml/ 2½ cups) brown stock

Chop the onion and fry gently in the butter.

Cut the steak and kidney into 1 inch (2.5 cm) cubes.

Season the flour with salt and pepper.

Toss the steak and kidney in the seasoned flour.

Brown on all sides in the remaining butter in the pan.

Arrange the steak, kidney, onion and mushrooms in a 2 pint (1.15 litre/ 5 cups) pie dish in layers.

Stir in remaining flour into the remaining butter in the pan.

Cook for a few minutes.

Gradually add the stock.

Pour into the pie dish, almost covering the meat.

Cover the pie dish with foil and bake for 1½ hours.

Remove from the oven and remove the foil.

Roll out the pastry and cover the pie dish, moistening the edges to seal.

Increase the oven temperature and bake for 25 minutes.

Oven: 300°F/150°C Gas Mark 2
Increase to: 400°F/200°C Gas Mark 6

STEAK AND KIDNEY PUDDING Serves 6

For the filling:
1½ lbs (675 g) rump steak
12 oz (350 g) ox kidney
A little salt and pepper
1 oz (25 g) flour
1 onion
¾ pint (450 ml/ 2 cups) brown stock

For the suet crust pastry:
8 oz (225 g) self-raising flour
A pinch of salt
4 oz (100 g) suet
About ¼ pint (150 ml/ ⅔ cup) water

To make the suet crust pastry:

Sift the flour and salt together.

Stir in the suet.

Gradually add enough water to make a soft dough.

Roll out two-thirds of the dough and, without stretching it, line a 2 pint (1.15 litre/ 5 cups) pudding basin.

To make the filling:

Remove the skin and fat from the steak and kidney.

Cut into 2 inch (5 cm) cubes.

Season the flour with salt and pepper.

Toss the steak and kideney in the flour.

Chop the onion.

Layer the steak, kidney and onion in the lined pudding basin.

Pour in the stock.

Roll out the remaining dough and cover the ingredients, moistening the edges to seal securely.

Cover with foil and tie a cloth over with string.

Stand the basin in a large saucepan with enough boiling water to come half way up the sides of the basin.

Steam for 3 hours.

MARKET HARBOROUGH PORK AND APPLE PIE

Serves 6

For the filling:
1½ lbs (675 g) pork
1 oz (25 g) flour
1 tablespoon oil
2 onions
2 sticks of celery
A little salt and pepper
¾ pint (450 ml/ 2 cups) stock
1 tablespoon Worcestershire sauce
3 large cooking apples

For the pastry:
8 oz (225 g) flour
4 oz (100 g) butter
A little water to mix
Milk or egg to glaze

To make the filling:

Trim any excess fat and gristle from the pork and cut into cubes.

Toss the meat in the flour and brown in the oil.

Remove the meat from the pan.

Slice the onions and celery and fry in the remaining oil until soft.

Season with a little salt and pepper.

Add the stock and the Worcestershire sauce.

Return the meat to the pan, cover and simmer for 30 minutes.

Peel, core and slice the cooking apples.

Place half of the sliced apple in a large pie dish.

Pour the pork, onion, celery and stock on to the apples in the pie dish.

Top with the remaining apple slices.

To make the pastry:

Rub the butter into the flour until the mixture resembles breadcrumbs.

Add enough cold water to make a soft dough.

Leave the dough to rest for 30 minutes.

Roll out the pastry and place over the ingredients in the pie dish, moistening the edges to seal.

Brush the pastry with the milk or egg to glaze.

Bake for 30 minutes.

Oven: 400°F/200°C Gas Mark 6

MELTON MOWBRAY PORK PIE

Pork pies have been made in Melton Mowbray for about 150 years. They are still being moulded by hand in the traditional way. The round shape is called a 'coffyn' or 'coffer'.

For the hot water crust pastry:
1 lb (450 g) flour
A pinch of salt
8 oz (225 g) lard
¼ pint (150 ml/ ⅔ cup) milk and water, mixed
1 egg

For the filling:
2 lbs (1 kg) boned pork (leg or shoulder)
1 pig's trotter or pork trimmings and bones
1 onion
1 bay leaf
1½ pint (900ml/ 3¾ cups) water
A pinch of dried sage
A little salt and pepper

To make the filling:

Prepare the filling before you make the pastry.

Put the pig's trotter or pork trimmings and bones into a large saucepan.

Chop the onion and put into the pan along with the bay leaf and the water.

Boil for 2 hours or until the stock is reduced to 1 pint (600 ml/ 2½ cups).

Cool and skim off the fat.

As the stock cools it should form a jelly.

Cut the pork meat into very small cubes.

Season the pork with salt, pepper and dried sage.

To make the pastry crust:

Sift the flour and salt together.

Rub half the lard into the flour.

Put the other half of the lard into a saucepan with the milk and water.

Bring to the boil then gradually add to the flour.

Stir well then knead until smooth.

The pastry must be raised while it is still warm.

Roll out ¾ of the pastry dough into a large circular shape about ½ inch (1 cm) thick.

Gently mould the pastry around a floured and greased round pot or cake tin.

Turn the pot or tin onto its side and roll it a few times to smooth the outsides and loosen the pastry.

Leave the pastry on the pot or tin for 15 minutes or until cool.

Remove the pastry case from the pot or tin.

Pack the pork meat into the pastry case.

Roll out the remaining pastry to make a lid for the pie.

Moisten the edges of the lid and press onto the case, crimping the edges to make a raised ridge.

Make a hole in the centre of the pastry lid, and brush the pie with beaten egg to glaze.

Bake at the higher temperature for 20 minutes then reduce the temperature and continue baking for 1½ hours.

Re-heat the stock until melted and pour it into the pie through the hole in the lid. Leave until cold before serving.

Oven: 400°F/200°C Gas Mark 6
Reduce to: 350°F/180°C Gas Mark 4

PORK AND APPLE PIE

Serves 4-6

This pie uses a potato topping rather than a true pastry.

For the filling:
1½ lbs (675 g) lean pork
1 lb (450 g) cooking apples
1 onion
½ pint (300 ml/ 1¼ cups) stock
A little salt and pepper

For the potato crust:
8 oz (225 g) self-raising flour
4 oz (100 g) butter
1 lb (450 g) potatoes
A pinch of salt
A little milk to glaze

To make the filling:

Cut the pork into cubes.

Peel, core and slice the cooking apples.

Chop the onion.

Layer the pork, apple and onions in a deep pie dish, beginning and ending with a layer of pork.

Sprinkle each layer of pork with a little salt and pepper.

Pour the stock over the layers.

To make the potato crust:

Cook the peeled potatoes until soft and then mash them.

Rub the butter into the flour.

Mix the mashed potato into the mixture.

Season with a little salt.

Knead the dough and roll out to a thickness of about 1½ inches (3.5 cm).

Cover the pie with the dough and brush with milk to glaze.

Bake for 1½ hours until the crust is golden brown.

Oven: 300°F/150°C Gas Mark 2

BACON AND COW-HEEL PIE

Serves 6

For the filling
1 dressed cow-heel
1 lb (450 g) bacon rashers
2 onions
1 oz (25 g) butter
1 pint (600 ml/ 2½ cups) brown stock

For the pastry:
8 oz (225 g) flour
4 oz (100 g) butter
A pinch of salt
A little cold water to mix
Milk to glaze

To make the filling:

Put the cow-heel in a large pan and cover with stock.

Bring to the boil, cover and simmer, for 3 hours until tender.

Strip the meat from the cow-heel and cut into cubes.

Wrap the meat in the bacon rashers.

Place the wrapped meat in a 2 pint (1.15 litre/ 5 cups) pie dish.

Slice the onions and gently fry in butter for 5 minutes, then put the onions into the pie dish with the meat.

To make the pastry:

Sift the flour and salt, and rub in the butter until the mixture resembles breadcrumbs.

Add enough cold water to make a soft dough.

Leave the pastry dough for 30 minutes then roll out and cover the meat and onion filling in the pie dish.

Brush with milk and bake for 1 hour.

Oven: 350°F/180°C Gas Mark 4

QUORN BACON ROLL

Serves 6

This dish was probably served after a hunt, to the 'stable hands' and the beaters.

1 lb (450 g) suet crust pastry
12 rashers of bacon, preferably collar
2 large onions
1 teaspoon chopped sage
Black pepper
1 tablespoon golden syrup

Roll out the suet crust pastry to make a large rectangle about ¼ inch (5 mm) thick.

Lay the rashers over the pastry to within about 1 inch (2.5 cm) of the edge.

Chop the onions and sprinkle over the bacon.

Sprinkle with sage and pepper.

Trickle the golden syrup along the middle.

Roll up the pastry like a Swiss roll and seal the edges together with water.

Wrap the roll in buttered foil then in a pudding cloth, lightly floured on both sides. Tie the ends with string.

Boil in water in a large saucepan for 2½ hours.

Lift out the roll, unwrap and place on an ovenproof serving dish.

Place in the oven for about 5 minutes to dry the outside.

Serve in thick slices, with potatoes, turnips and carrots.

Oven: 350°F/180°C Gas Mark 4

FAGGOTS

Serves 4

Traditionally, faggots are cooked in small squares of pig's caul which is part of the animal's stomach (available from butchers). Balls of the mixture are wrapped in the caul squares and are then put into a roasting tin with the joins underneath.

1 lb (450 g) pig's liver
½ pint (300 ml/ 1¼ cups) milk
4 oz (100 g) fat pork
1 onion
2 eggs
A large pinch of grated nutmeg
A little salt and pepper
6 oz (175 g) breadcrumbs
Beef stock to mix

Soak the liver in milk for at least an hour.

Mince the liver, pork and onion.

Beat the eggs and add the grated nutmeg, salt and pepper.

Stir in the liver mixture.

Work in the breadcrumbs to give a stiff consistency, adding a little stock if more liquid is required.

Press into a greased baking tin, or wrap in squares of pig's caul.

Cover with tin foil.

Bake for about 45 minutes until browned.

Oven: 375°F/190°C Gas Mark 5

MARKET DAY SAVOURY

Serves 4-6

This dish was left cooking while the farmer's wife went to the market. The longer it cooked the better was the flavour.

1½ lbs (675 g) potatoes
4 onions
1 apple
2 pig's kidneys
8 oz (225 g) tomatoes
6 pork chops
1 teaspoon dried sage
1 tablespoon tomato purée
½ pint (300 ml/ 1¼ cups) stock

Peel and slice the potatoes and onions.

Slice the kidneys.

Peel, core and chop the apple.

Skin and chop the tomatoes.

In a large saucepan or a flameproof casserole layer the potatoes, onions, pork chops, kidneys and tomatoes, beginning and ending with a layer of potatoes.

Sprinkle the apple, sage and tomato purée between the layers.

Pour the stock over and cover with a tightly fitting lid.

Simmer gently for 2½-3 hours, or bake in the oven for 2-4 hours.

Oven: 300°F/150°C Gas Mark 2

WHITE PUDDING

Makes about 2 lbs (900 g)

This pudding is a paler version of the familiar black pudding. It has a milder flavour and is made without the pig's blood.

6 oz (175 g) medium oatmeal
3 oz (75 g) round grain rice
3 oz (75 g) barley
2½ pints (1.4 litres/ 6¼ cups) milk and water mixed
12 oz (350 g) pork fat
2 onions
2 eggs
A little salt and pepper
1 teaspoon dried sage

Put the oatmeal, rice and barley in a large saucepan.

Add the milk and water.

Bring to the boil and simmer for about 30 minutes until the grains are tender. The consistency should be similiar to porridge.

Chop up the pork fat and onions.

Add to the grains.

Beat the eggs, add to the mixture and mix well.

Season with salt, pepper and sage.

Turn into a well greased baking tin and bake for 50 minutes to 1 hour until firm.

Serve in slices, fried with bacon for breakfast.

Oven:350°F/180°C Gas Mark 4

BLACK PUDDING

Black puddings are popular in the Midlands. The skins used for the pudding mixture are brushed with blood before cooking, to give the puddings their characteristic black colour.

8 oz (225 g) fresh breadcrumbs
4 oz (100 g) barley
4 oz (100 g) medium oatmeal
1 lb (450 g) pork fat
4 onions
A large pinch of salt and pepper
½ teaspoon dried sage
1 pint (600 ml/ 2½ cups) pig's blood

Soak the breadcrumbs in water for a few minutes.

Squeeze dry.

Put the barley and oatmeal into a saucepan and cover with water.

Bring to the boil and simmer for about 30 minutes until the barley is tender. The consistency should be similar to porridge.

Remove from the heat and add the breadcrumbs.

Finely chop the pork fat and the onions.

Stir into the grain mixture.

Season with salt, pepper and sage.

Add the pig's blood and mix well.

Turn into a well greased baking tin.

Bake for about 1 hour until firm.

Serve in slices, fried for breakfast with bacon and sausages or add to a Hot Pot.

Oven: 350°F/180°C Gas Mark 4

STILTON FLAN

Serves 6

For the pastry:
6 oz (175 g) flour
A pinch of salt
3 oz (75 g) butter
A little cold water

For the filling:
2 onions
1 oz (25 g) butter
6 oz (175 g) Stilton cheese
3 eggs
¼ pint (150 ml/ ⅔ cup) single cream
A little salt and pepper

To make the pastry:

Sift the flour and salt.

Rub the butter into the flour until the mixture resembles breadcrumbs.

Add enough water to make a soft dough.

Roll out the dough and line a flan dish with it.

Bake blind at the higher temperature for 10 minutes.

To make the filling:

Chop the onions and fry in the butter until soft but not brown.

Crumble the Stilton cheese.

Place the onions and cheese into the partly baked pastry case.

Beat the eggs and the cream together and season with a little salt and pepper.

Pour into the flan.

Reduce the oven temperature and bake for about 40 minutes or until the filling has set.

Serve hot or cold.

Oven: 400°F/200°C Gas Mark 6
Reduce to: 350°F/180°C Gas Mark 4

STILTON SAVOURY

Serves 4

4 slices of bread
1 bunch of watercress
2 ripe William pears
6 oz (175 g) Stilton cheese
A little cayenne pepper

Toast the bread on both sides.

Chop the watrercress, discarding any yellowing leaves.

Thinly slice the pears.

Thinly slice the Stilton cheese.

Arrange the toast in a greased dish and top each slice with first the watercress then the pears then the cheese.

Sprinkle with a little cayenne pepper.

Bake for 5 minutes.

Serve immediately.

Oven: 350°F/180°C Gas Mark 4

LEICESTER CROUSTADES

Serves 4

8 oz (225 g) cooked haddock
¼ pint (150 ml/ ⅔ cup) white sauce
2 oz (50 g) Red Leicester cheese
1 oz (25 g) butter
1 tablespoon cream
A little salt and pepper
A pinch of cayenne pepper
4 bread rolls

Cut the top off each roll and scoop out the bread from inside each one.

Flake the haddock and mix with the white sauce.

Grate the cheese and add to the mixture.

Add the cream.

Season with a little salt, pepper and cayenne pepper.

Mix well.

Pile the mixture into the bread roll cases and replace the lids.

Brush the outside of the rolls with melted butter to glaze.

Bake in the oven for 15 minutes to crisp the rolls.

Oven: 350°F/180°C Gas Mark 4

LEICESTERSHIRE RAREBIT

Serves 4

Leicestershire rarebit is otherwise known as Leicestershire Rare-bite or Rabbit. It was originally made by toasting a slice of bread in front of the fire, soaking this in beer and red wine and then covering it with thinly sliced cheese. The toast was then left in front of the fire until the cheese had melted.

4-8 slices of bread
8 oz (225 g) Red Leicester cheese
1 oz (25 g) butter
A little milk
A pinch of salt and pepper
1 teaspoon made-up English mustard

Toast the bread.

Melt the butter.

Grate the cheese and add to the butter.

Heat gently until the cheese has melted.

Add enough milk to make a spreading consistency.

Season with salt, pepper and mustard.

Brown under a hot grill and serve immediately.

PLOUGHMAN'S LUNCH

This meal is named after the farm workers who took it to work, to eat at midday with a glass of beer. It is now served in public houses at lunch time.

1 small cottage loaf
4 oz (100 g) Red Leicester cheese
A few pickled onions

Serve these together with butter and a side salad.

LEICESTERSHIRE CHEESE AND HAM PUDDING

Serves 6

8 slices of bread
8 oz (225 g) Red Leicester cheese
6 oz (175 g) ham
1 oz (25 g) butter
1 large onion
3 sticks of celery
½ pint (300 ml/ 1¼ cups) milk
3 eggs
1 teaspoon mustard powder
A little salt and pepper

Chop the onion and celery and fry in the butter until soft.

Beat the milk, eggs, mustard powder, salt and pepper together.

Grate the cheese. Reserve a little for the topping.

Remove the crusts from the slices of bread and dip them into the milk and egg mxiture.

Chop the ham.

Layer the onion, celery, cheese, ham and slices of bread in a greased, large, shallow ovenproof dish, beginning and ending with a layer of bread.

Pour over any remaining milk mixture and sprinkle with grated cheese.

Bake for about 45 minutes or until the top is golden.

Oven: 350°F/180°C Gas Mark 4

MUSHROOM GRATIN

Serves 4

8 oz (225 g) mushrooms
8 oz (225 g) red lentils
1 oz (25 g) butter
2 oz (50 g) breadcrumbs
2 oz (50 g) Red Leicester cheese
1 bay leaf
A pinch of paprika pepper
A pinch of salt and freshly ground black pepper

Wash the lentils and put into a saucepan with enough water to cover.

Add the bay leaf and boil for 15 minutes.

Drain.

Wash and slice the mushrooms and gently cook in the butter.

Put the lentils in a greased ovenproof dish and arrange the mushrooms on top.

Sprinkle with paprika pepper, salt and freshly ground black pepper.

Grate the cheese and mix with the breadcrumbs.

Sprinkle the mixture over the mushrooms.

Bake for 20-30 minutes.

Oven: 350°F/180°C Gas Mark 4

BRUSSELS SPROUTS GRATINÉE

Serves 6

1½ lbs (675 g) Brussels sprouts
6 rashers of streaky bacon
3 oz (75 g) cheese
1 oz (25 g) breadcrumbs

Boil the Brussels sprouts in water for 15 minutes until tender.

Drain and keep on one side.

Chop the bacon and fry for about 10 minutes until cooked.

Place the bacon in an ovenproof dish.

Toss the Brussels sprouts in the bacon fat in the pan.

Add to the bacon in the ovenproof dish.

Grate the cheese and mix with the breadcrumbs.

Sprinkle on top of the sprouts and bacon.

Place under a hot grill to brown.

Serve as a starter or with cold meat as a main course.

BACON AND BEANS Serves 6

The savory in this traditional cottage dish enhances the flavour of the broad beans.

12 oz (350 g) gammon rashers
2 glasses red wine
1 tablespoon sugar
A few cloves
3 lbs (1.5 kg) young broad beans, shelled
4 oz (100 g) butter
A tablespoon freshly chopped parsley
1 tablespoon freshly chopped savory

Put the gammon rashers in a saucepan.

Add the wine, sugar and a few cloves.

Add enough water to cover the gammon.

Bring to the boil and simmer for 20 minutes until the gammon is tender.

Remove the gammon from the saucepan and cut each rasher into about 8 pieces.

Cook the beans in boiling water for about 15 minutes until tender.

Drain the beans and pile them on to the middle of a serving dish which should be kept hot.

Arrange the gammon round the beans.

Melt the butter and add the parsley and savory.

Pour the flavoured butter over the gammon and beans and serve immediately.

BROAD BEAN TART

Serves 6

This recipe dates from the 17th century.

For the pastry:
6 oz (175 g) flour
A pinch of salt
3 oz (75 g) butter
A little cold water

For the filling:
8 oz (225 g) fresh or frozen broad beans
1 cooking apple
4 oz (100 g) ham
3 eggs
1 teaspoon made-up mustard
A little salt and pepper
½ pint (300 ml/ 1¼ cups) cider

To make the pastry:

Sift the flour and salt together.

Rub the butter into the flour until the mixture resembles breadcrumbs.

Add enough cold water to make a soft dough.

Leave to rest for 30 minutes.

Roll out and line an 8 inch (20 cm) flan ring.

Bake blind for 10 minutes at the higher temperature.

To make the filling:

Cook the beans in water until tender.

Peel, core and dice the apple.

Dice the ham.

Beat the eggs with the mustard, salt and pepper.

Add the cider and beat well.

Put the beans, apple and ham in the pastry case.

Pour the egg and cider mixture over.

Bake for 50 minutes, until set, at the lower oven temperature.

Serve warm or cold.

Oven: 400°F/200°C Gas Mark 6
Reduce to: 325°F/160°C Gas Mark 3

PEASE PUDDING

Serves 6

This is a Victorian recipe. It was believed that 'a full belly to the labourer is the foundation of public morals and the only real source of public peace'. It is traditionally served with roast pork.

1 lb (450 g) dried split green peas
6 oz (175 g) bacon or ham
1 onion
2 pints (1.15 litres/ 5 cups) ham stock
3 oz (75 g) butter
2 egg yolks
A little salt and pepper

Dice the bacon or ham and chop the onion finely.

Put the peas, bacon or ham, onion and stock in a saucepan.

Bring to the boil and simmer for 45 minutes until the peas are tender and rather mushy.

Beat in the butter and the egg yolks.

Season with a little salt and pepper.

Serve with butter and gravy.

APPLE MERINGUE FLAN

Serves 4

For the pastry:
6 oz (175 g) flour
3 oz (75 g) butter

For the filling:
1 lb (450 g) cooking apples
2 oz (50 g) caster sugar

For the topping:
2 egg whites
1 oz (25 g) caster sugar

To make the pastry:

Rub the butter into the flour until the mixture resembles breadcrumbs.

Add enough cold water to make a soft dough.

Leave to rest for about 30 minutes.

Roll out the dough and line a pie dish.

Bake blind for 10 minutes.

To make the filling:

Peel, core and slice the apples.

Put them into a saucepan with the sugar and a very little water.

Cook gently for 15 to 20 minutes until the apples are soft.

Pour the filling into the pastry case.

To make the topping:

Whisk the egg whites until stiff.

Fold in the sugar and spread the mixture onto the apple in the pie dish.

Bake for 5 to 10 minutes to brown the topping.

Serve hot or cold.

Oven: 400°F/200°C Gas Mark 6

TREACLE TART

Serves 6-8

In the 18th century this tart was made with black treacle, currants, peel and spices.

For the pastry:
8 oz (225 g) flour
A pinch of salt
4 oz (100 g) butter
A little cold water to mix
A little milk to glaze

For the filling:
8 rounded tablespoons golden syrup
4 oz (100 g) fresh breadcrumbs
Grated rind of 1 lemon
1 tablespoon lemon juice
A large pinch of ground ginger

To make the pastry:

Sift the flour and salt.

Rub in the butter until the mixture resembles breadcrumbs.

Add enough water to make a soft dough.

Leave to rest for 30 minutes.

Roll out ¾ of the pastry dough and line a 10 inch (25 cm) flan dish.

To make the filling:

Warm the syrup in a saucepan and add the lemon rind and juice.

Stir in the breadcrumbs and the ground ginger.

Pour into the pastry case.

Roll out the remaining pastry, cut into strips and make into a lattice pattern over the filling.

Brush with milk to glaze.

Bake for 30 minutes.

Serve hot or cold.

Oven: 400°F/200°C Gas Mark 6

BLACK TREACLE ROLL

Serves 4-6

8 oz (225 g) self-raising flour
A pinch of salt
4 oz (100 g) shredded suet
2 oz (50 g) granulated sugar
4 oz (100 g) treacle
4 oz (100 g) chopped dried fruit
½ teaspoon ground ginger

Sift the flour and salt into a large mixing basin.

Add the shredded suet and the sugar.

Add enough cold water to make an elastic dough and knead lightly for about a minute.

Roll out the dough into an 8-10 inch (20-25 cm) long rectangle ¼ inch (5 mm) thick.

Mix the treacle with the chopped dried fruit and ground ginger.

Spread the mixture over the dough to within 1 inch (2.5 cm) of the edges.

Moisten the edges with water and roll up like a Swiss roll.

Place in a greased dish with the join underneath.

Bake for 30 minutes

Serve hot with warmed treacle.

Oven: 400°F/200°C Gas Mark 6

TREACLE PUDDING

Serves 6

Steamed puddings were very popular in Victorian times. They were boiled in a cloth which was well buttered and floured. The mixture was tied loosely in the cloth to allow for some expansion.

2 oz (50 g) fresh breadcrumbs
4 oz (100 g) flour
½ teaspoon baking powder
3 oz (75 g) shredded suet
2 oz (50 g) caster sugar
3 tablespoons golden syrup
1 egg
¼ pint (150 ml/ ⅔ cup) milk
Extra golden syrup
1 tablespoon lemon juice

Mix the breadcrumbs, flour, baking powder, suet and sugar together.

Warm the golden syrup and add to the mixture.

Beat the egg and stir it in.

Add enough milk to make a soft, dropping consistency.

Turn into a well greased 1½ pint (900ml/ 3¾ cups) pudding basin.

Cover with greaseproof paper and foil and tie down with string.

Put the basin into a large saucepan with enough boiling water to come half way up the sides of the basin.

Steam for 1½ hours, topping up with water if necessary.

Turn out and serve with more warmed golden syrup mixed with a little lemon juice.

FIG PIE

Serves 6-8

For the pastry:
12 oz (350 g) flour
6 oz (175 g) butter
2 egg yolks
1 oz (25 g) caster sugar

For the filling:
8 oz (225 g) dried figs
2 oz (50 g) golden syrup
A large pinch of mixed spice
2 teaspoons cornflour
2 oz (50 g) currants

To make the pastry:

Rub the butter into the flour until the mixture resembles breadcrumbs.

Mix in the caster sugar.

Beat the egg yolks and add to the mixture.

If necessary, add a little cold water to make a soft dough.

Leave to rest for 30 minutes.

Line an 8 inch (20 cm) flan ring with ⅔ of the pastry.

To make the filling:

Soak the figs in water overnight.

Put the figs in a saucepan with the golden syrup and the mixed spice.

Cover with water.

Bring to the boil and simmer until the figs are tender.

Blend the cornflour with a little cold water and add to the figs.

Cook until the mixture thickens.

Add the currants.

Pour the mixture into the pastry case.

Roll out the remaining pastry and cover the filling, moistening the edges to seal.

Bake for 10 minutes at the higher temperature, then lower the temperature and continue cooking for 30 minutes.

Oven: 425°F/220°C Gas Mark 7
Reduce to: 350°F/180°C Gas Mark 4

FRUIT AND BREAD PUDDING

Serves 4

4 slices of bread
¼ pint (150 ml/ ⅔ cup) milk
2 oz (50 g) flour
A pinch of salt
1 teaspoon mixed spice
8 oz (225 g) dried mixed fruit
3 oz (75 g) caster sugar
3 oz (75 g) butter

Soak the bread in the milk for 20 minutes.

Remove the bread from the milk and squeeze out any excess liquid.

Sift the flour, salt and mixed spice together.

Mix in the bread and mash well.

Add the dried fruit and the sugar.

Melt the butter and pour into the mixture.

Mix well.

Turn into a well greased ovenproof dish and bake for 1½ hours.

Oven: 375°F/190°C Gas Mark 5

BOILED APPLE PUDDING

Serves 4

8 oz (225 g) cooking apples
6 oz (175 g) breadcrumbs
8 oz (225 g) currants
3 eggs
2 oz (50 g) sugar
2 oz (50 g) butter
2 tablespoons brandy
Grated rind of ½ lemon

Peel, core and slice the apples.

Mix in the breadcrumbs and currants.

Beat the eggs with the sugar and add to the mixture.

Melt the butter and stir it in.

Add the brandy and lemon rind.

Mix the ingredients together.

Turn into a greased 2 pint (1.15 litres/ 5 cups) pudding basin.

Cover with foil and a cloth and tie down with string.

Place the basin in a saucepan with enough boiling water to come half way up the sides of the basin.

Steam for 2½ to 3 hours, topping up with water if necessary.

LEICESTER PUDDING

Serves 6-8

8 oz (225 g) self-raising flour
4 oz (100 g) butter
4 oz (100 g) caster sugar
2 eggs
A little milk
8 oz (225 g) jam

Sift the flour and rub in the butter until the mixture resembles breadcrumbs.

Add the sugar.

Beat the eggs and add to the mixture.

Add enough milk to make a soft dropping consistency.

Grease a large pudding basin and spread the jam over the base and the sides.

Spoon on the mixture.

Cover with greaseproof paper and then foil.

Tie the foil down with string.

Place the pudding basin in a large saucepan filled with enough water to come halfway up the sides of the basin.

Steam for 2 hours.

Turn out and serve with extra warmed jam and cream.

MIXED FRUIT STIR-ABOUT

Serves 4

This old farmhouse recipe can be made with many kinds of fruit in season from the garden or from the hedgerows such as rhubarb, gooseberries, raspberries, blackberries and black currants.

8 oz (225 g) fruit
4 oz (100 g) flour
2 oz (50 g) butter
A pinch of salt
2 oz (50 g) caster sugar
½ pint (300 ml/ 1¼ cups) milk

Prepare the fruit by washing, top and tailing if necessary, and chopping.

Rub the butter into the flour until the mixture resembles breadcrumbs.

Add a pinch of salt and the sugar.

Mix well.

Gradully pour in the milk until a thick batter is made.

Add the prepared fruit and stir about.

Pour into a greased ovenproof dish.

Bake for 40 minutes.

Serve hot with cream.

Oven: 400°F/200°C Gas Mark 6

PARADISE PUDDING

If you'd have a good pudding
Pray mind what you're taught
Take two pennyworth of eggs
When they are twelve for a groat
Take of that summer fruit
Which Eve once did cozen
Well pared and well grated
At least half a dozen
Six ounces of bread
Let your maids eat the crust
The crumbs must be grated
As fine as small dust
Six ounces of currants
But pray pick them clean
Lest they grate in your teeth
You know what I mean
And if you've a mind
To be clever and handy
Put in good lemon rind
And a large glass of brandy
Six ounces of sugar
Won't make it too sweet
With some salt and some nutmeg
To make it complete
Three hours let it boil
Without fuss or flutter
And then serve it up
With some good melted butter
Adam tasted the pudding
'Twas wonderous nice
So Eve cut her husband another large slice.

PARADISE PUDDING

Serves 3-4

3 large cooking apples
3 oz (75 g) breadcrumbs
3 oz (75 g) currants
3 oz (75 g) caster sugar
Grated rind of 1 lemon
A pinch of salt
A pinch of grated nutmeg
2 eggs
½ wineglass brandy
3 oz (75 g) melted butter

Peel, core and grate the apples.

Add the breadcrumbs, currants, sugar, lemon rind, salt and grated nutmeg and mix well.

Beat the eggs until light and frothy then add to the mixture.

Stir in the brandy.

Turn into a greased pudding basin.

Cover with greaseproof paper and then foil.

Tie down with string.

Place in a saucepan with enough water to come half way up the sides of the pudding basin.

Steam for 1½ hours.

Serve with melted butter.

CHARTER PUDDING

Serve 4

This delicious custard has been adapted from a recipe known to have been made in 1821.

Grated rind of 1 lemon
1 pint (600 ml/ 2½ cups) single cream
4 eggs
2 oz (50 g) caster sugar
2 fresh apricots

Mix the grated lemon rind with the cream.

Beat the eggs with the sugar and add to the cream.

Pour the mixture into a greased ovenproof dish.

Bake for about 30 minutes or until the top has browned.

Leave to cool.

Peel the apricots and slice.

Arrange the apricot slices on top of the cooled pudding and serve.

Oven: 400°F/200°C Gas Mark 6

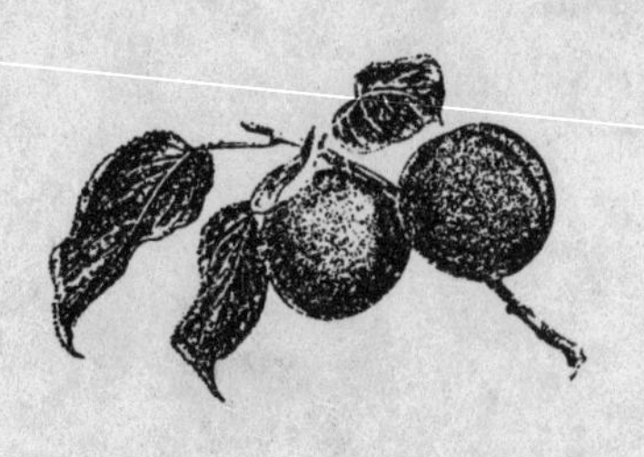

COURTING CAKE

8 oz (225 g) self-raising flour
4 oz (100 g) butter
3 oz (75 g) caster sugar
1 egg
About 3 or 4 tablespoons raspberry or strawberry jam
Milk to glaze
Icing sugar

Rub the butter into the flour until the mixture resembles breadcrumbs.

Add the sugar and bind the mixture with the well beaten egg.

Roll out and line a pie plate with half the pastry dough.

Roll out the remaining pastry dough and place on top, moistening and crimping the edges to seal.

Prick the top with a fork and brush with milk to glaze.

Bake for 25 minutes or until the top is golden brown.

Dredge with icing sugar and leave to cool.

Cut into slices to serve.

Oven: 400°F/200°C Gas Mark 6

WHETSTONE CAKES

12 oz (350 g) self-raising flour
4 oz (100 g) caster sugar
4 oz (100 g) butter
2 eggs
1 teaspoon caraway seeds
Rose water

Cream together the butter and the sugar until pale and fluffy.

Gradually beat in the eggs.

Add the caraway seeds.

Fold in the flour.

Add enough rose water to make a soft but not sticky dough.

Knead the dough until smooth.

Roll out the dough very thinly and cut out circles 2 inches (5 cm) in diameter.

Place the circles of dough on greased baking trays.

Prick each one with a fork.

Bake for 20 minutes.

Oven: 325°F/160°C Gas Mark 3

PUMP CAKE

This cake originates in the days when water had to be pumped at the kitchen sink.

2 oz (50 g) butter
3 oz (75 g) caster sugar
1 egg
A few drops of almond essence
1 oz (25 g) ground almonds
4 oz (100 g) self-raising flour
½ teaspoon baking powder
3 tablespoons apricot jam

Beat together the butter and sugar until pale and fluffy.

Gradually add the egg and beat well.

Add a few drops of almond essence.

Stir in the ground almonds.

Sift the flour and the baking powder and stir into the cake mixture to make a soft dough.

Divide the mixture in half.

Press half into a greased and lined sandwich tin.

Spread with jam.

Press the remaining dough on top.

Run the cake under cold water. (This would originally have been done under the pump.)

Drain off the water.

Sprinkle with caster sugar and bake for 30 minutes.

Oven: 350°F/180°C Gas Mark 4

HUNTSMAN'S CAKE

A cake which was traditionally eaten for tea, after a day's hunting.

4 oz (100 g) butter
4 oz (100 g) caster sugar
4 eggs
8 oz (225 g) self-raising flour
4 oz (100 g) ground almonds
8 oz (225 g) mixed dried fruit
2 oz (50 g) glacé cherries
2 oz (50 g) flaked almonds
½ pint (300 ml/ 1¼ cups) sherry
1 teaspoon bicarbonate of soda
1 tablespoon vinegar

Separate the eggs.

Cream together the butter and sugar until pale and fluffy.

Add the egg yolks one by one, beating well each time.

Add the flour, ground almonds, dried fruit, cherries and flaked almonds.

Stir in half of the sherry.

Dissolve the bicarbonate of soda in the vinegar and stir into the cake mixture.

Beat the egg whites until stiff and fold them in.

Turn into a greased and lined 8 inch (20 cm) cake tin.

Cover with greaseproof paper.

Bake for 10 minutes at the higher temperature.

Lower the temperature and continue cooking for a further 2 hours.

Remove the cake from the oven and pour the rest of the sherry over while it is still hot.

Leave the cake in the tin, covered with a cloth, until cold.

Oven: 400°F/200°C Gas Mark 6
Reduce to: 325°F/160°C Gas Mark 3

BELVOIR CASTLE BUNS

These buns, which are a Rutland version of Chelsea buns, were apparently popular with the VII Duke of Rutland (1818-1906).

¼ pint (150 ml/ ⅔ cup) milk and water mixed
½ oz (15 g) fresh yeast
4 oz (100 g) sugar
1 lb (450 g) flour
1 teaspoon salt
2 oz (50 g) butter
4 oz (100 g) chopped mixed dried fruit
Milk to glaze

Warm the milk and water and crumble in the yeast.

Add 1 teaspoon of the sugar and stir until dissolved.

Leave the yeast mixture to stand in a warm place for 15 minutes until frothy.

Sift the flour and the salt.

Rub in the butter and add the remaining sugar.

Pour in the yeast mixture and mix well.

Add half of the dried fruit.

Knead on a floured surface for about 10 minutes until the dough is smooth and elastic.

Place in a bowl and cover with a damp cloth.

Leave in a warm place until doubled in size.

Knock back the dough and knead again.

Roll out the dough to make a square ½ inch (1 cm) thick.

Sprinkle with the remaining dried fruit and roll up like a Swiss roll.

Cut the roll into pieces 1 inch (2.5 cm) wide.

Place the pieces on greased baking sheets with the cut side uppermost.

Leave in a warm place for about 30 minutes to prove.

Brush with milk to glaze and bake for 10 minutes.

Oven: 425°F/220°C Gas Mark 7

BOSWORTH JUMBLES

These small cakes are said to have been dropped from the pocket of King Richard III's cook on the battlefield of Bosworth.

6 oz (175 g) butter
6 oz (175 g) caster sugar
1 egg
1 teaspoon grated lemon rind
8 oz (225 g) flour

Cream the butter and sugar together until light and fluffy.

Beat in the egg and the grated lemon rind.

Gradually sieve in the flour and mix to a stiff consistency.

Make small pieces of the dough into 'S' shapes.

Place on greased baking trays.

Bake for 20 minutes.

Cool on a wire rack.

Oven: 350°F/180°C Gas Mark 4

PLUM SHUTTLES

These are shaped like weavers' shuttles — hence the name.

1 lb (450 g) flour
A pinch of salt
3 oz (75 g) lard
3 oz (75 g) caster sugar
6 oz (175 g) currants
1 beaten egg
½ oz (15 g) fresh yeast
1 teaspoon caster sugar
¼ pint (150 ml/ ⅔ cup) warm water

Sift the flour and the salt.

Rub in the lard.

Mix in the sugar, currants and beaten egg.

Cream the yeast with a teaspoon of sugar and the warm water.

Stir into the flour to make a soft dough.

Knead the dough for 10 minutes.

Place the dough in a greased bowl and cover with a clean, damp cloth.

Leave in a warm place until doubled in size.

Knock back and knead again lightly.

Divide the dough into small pieces and shape each piece into an oval shape, like a weaver's shuttle.

Place on greased baking sheets, cover and leave in a warm place for 20 minutes to prove.

Bake for 15 minutes.

Oven: 425°F/220°C Gas Mark 7

LEICESTER CHEESECAKES

Makes 12

12 oz (350 g) puff pastry
2 oz (50 g) butter
2 oz (50 g) caster sugar
1 egg
4 oz (100 g) curd cheese
2 oz (50 g) cake crumbs
2 oz (50 g) currants
1 tablespoon single cream
A little grated nutmeg
Grated rind of 1 lemon
1 tablespoon brandy

Roll out the pastry thinly, and line 12 deep patty tins.

Cream the butter and the sugar until light and fluffy.

Beat in the egg and the curd cheese.

Add the cake crumbs, currants and single cream.

Add a little grated nutmeg, the grated lemon rind and the brandy.

Beat well to combine.

Fill the pastry cases with the mixture, but not right up to the brim.

Bake at the higher temperature for 15 minutes.

Reduce the oven temperature and continue cooking for a further 15 minutes or until the filling is firm to the touch.

Serve hot or cold with cream.

Oven: 400°F/200°C Gas Mark 6
Reduce to: 325°F/160°F/ Gas Mark 3

BRANDY SNAPS

Makes about 20

These were often served at fairs in the 16th and 17th centuries, sometimes in a tube shape, sometimes flat.

2 oz (50 g) golden syrup
2 oz (50 g) butter
2 oz (50 g) sugar
2 oz (50 g) flour
A pinch of salt
1 teaspoon ground ginger
A few drops of lemon juice
1 teaspoon brandy

Warm the syrup and add the butter and sugar.

Stir over a low heat until the butter has melted and the sugar has dissolved.

Remove from the heat and add the flour, salt, ground ginger, lemon juice and brandy.

Line two baking sheets with buttered greaseproof paper.

Put a few teaspoons of the mixture onto one baking sheet, spacing them well apart to allow for spreading.

Bake for 8-10 minutes until lacey and golden.

Leave for about 10 seconds then remove from the baking sheet with a palette knife.

If tubes are required, shape around a wooden spoon handle while the brandy snaps are still soft.

If the mixture hardens too quickly, return them to the oven for a couple of minutes to soften.

Put a few teaspoons of the brandy snap mixture on to the second baking tray and bake in the same way.

Store the brandy snaps in an air-tight tin.

Oven: 400°F/200°C Gas Mark 6

HUNTER NUTS

8 oz (225 g) plain flour
1 teaspoon ground ginger
4 oz (100 g) butter
3 oz (75 g) caster sugar
1 tablespoon treacle
1 egg

Sieve the flour and the ginger together.

Rub in the butter until the mixture resembles breadcrumbs.

Add the sugar.

Warm the treacle and beat with the egg.

Mix into the dry ingredients.

Make small round marble-sized balls with the mixture.

Place the balls on a greased baking sheet, well spaced to allow for considerable spread.

Bake for 30 minutes.

Oven: 325°F/160°C Gas Mark 3

COTTAGE LOAVES

Makes 4

3 lbs (1.5 kg) flour
1 tablespoon salt
1 oz (25 g) lard
2 oz (50 g) fresh yeast/ 1 oz (25 g) dried yeast
2 teaspoons sugar
1½ pints (900ml/ 3¾ cups) warm water
A little salted water
1 egg, beaten

Cream the yeast with the sugar and add to the water which should be hand hot.

Leave for 10 minutes in a warm place until frothy.

Sift the flour and salt and rub in the lard.

Add the yeast liquid and mix to make a dough.

Knead for 10 minutes or until the dough is smooth and elastic.

Put the dough in a greased bowl and cover with a clean, damp cloth.

Leave in a warm place for about an hour until the dough has doubled in size.

Knock back and knead lightly.

Divide the dough into 4 equal pieces.

Divide each piece into 2 pieces, one twice as big as the other.

Shape the larger pieces into rounds and place on greased baking trays.

Brush these pieces with salted water and place the smaller pieces one on each larger piece.

Press the floured handle of a wooden spoon in the centre of each loaf.

Brush each loaf with beaten egg to glaze.

Bake the loaves at the higher temperature for 5 minutes.

Reduce the temperature and continue baking for 30 minutes, until the loaves are golden brown. They should sound hollow when tapped on the base.

Oven: 450°F/230°C Gas Mark 8
Reduce to: 400°F/200°C Gas Mark 6

WHITE GINGERBREAD

1 lb (450 g) flour
12 oz (350 g) caster sugar
8 oz (225 g) butter
1 oz (25 g) ground ginger
1 oz (25 g) chopped candied peel
2 eggs

Melt the butter.

Stir in the sugar and heat gently until it dissolves.

Mix in the flour, ground ginger and the chopped peel.

Beat the eggs and add.

Mix well to make a soft dough.

Roll out to a thickness of ¼ inch (5 mm) and cut out shapes or press into a greased baking tin.

Bake for 15-20 minutes.

Oven: 375°F/190°C Gas Mark 5

HARVEST TRIPLE PLAIT

1 oz (25 g) fresh yeast/ ½ oz (15 g) dried yeast
15 fl oz (450 ml/ 2 cups) warm water
1 teaspoon sugar
1½ lbs (675 g) bread flour
1 teaspoon salt
½ oz (15 g) butter
1 oz (25 g) soft brown sugar
Cracked wheat

Crumble the yeast and dissolve it in the warm water.

Add a teaspoon of sugar.

Whisk the liquid with a fork and leave to stand for 10-15 minutes in a warm place until frothy.

Mix the flour and the salt together.

Rub in the butter and add the soft brown sugar.

Add the yeast liquid and mix to a dough.

Knead for about 10 minutes on a floured surface until the dough is smooth and elastic.

Place the dough in a lightly greased bowl and cover with a damp cloth, then leave in a warm place until doubled in size.

Knead again and divide into two equal pieces.

Divide one of the pieces into 3 and shape each piece into a strand about 20 inches (50 cm) long.

Plait the strands, moistening the ends to seal them together.

Divide the second piece of dough into 2, one slightly larger than the other.

The larger of the two pieces should make three 16 inch (40 cm) strands.

The smaller of the two pieces should make three 14 inch (36 cm) strands.

Plait the strands and moisten the ends to seal.

You should have 3 plaits of different sizes.

Place the large plait on a greased baking tray, brush with water and put the medium plait on top, making sure the ends stick together.

Brush with water and place the smallest plait on top.

Brush with water and sprinkle with cracked wheat.

Cover the triple plait with a damp cloth and leave in a warm place until doubled in size.

Bake for 45 minutes.

Oven: 425°F/220°C Gas Mark 7

PICKLED ONIONS

2 lbs (1 kg) small pickling or silverskin onions
2 oz (50 g) salt
2 pints (1.15 litres/ 5 cups) white wine vinegar
2 oz (50 g) mixed pickling spices
4 oz (100 g) sugar
2-3 sprigs fresh tarragon

Top and tail the pickling onions.

Put the onions in a bowl and pour boiling water over them.

Leave for 30 seconds.

Drain and cover with cold water.

Remove the skins under water.

Drain and sprinkle with the salt.

Cover with a clean cloth and leave overnight.

Rinse and drain the onions.

Pack into clean, dry jars.

Put a sprig of tarragon into each jar.

Put the vinegar, mixed spices (tied in a muslin bag) and sugar in a saucepan.

Bring to the boil and simmer for 5 minutes.

Remove the spices.

Pour the vinegar over the onions in the jars to cover.

Seal the jars and store for 3 weeks before using.

PICKLED MUSHROOMS

1 lb (450 g) small, button mushrooms
½ pint (300 ml/ 1¼ cups) white wine vinegar
A small stick of cinnamon
A few white peppercorns
A pinch of mace
A few cloves
A pinch of allspice
A small onion
1 teaspoon salt
½ teaspoon ground ginger
A few sprigs of thyme
A pinch of black pepper
4 tablespoons sherry

Put the cinnamon, white peppercorns, mace, cloves and allspice in a muslin bag.

Put the muslin bag into the white vinegar in a bottle or jar and leave for 6 weeks before using.

Remove the muslin bag and strain the vinegar.

Put the vinegar in a saucepan with the salt, ginger, thyme, and black pepper.

Chop the onion and add to the vinegar.

Wash and add the mushrooms.

Cover the pan and cook gently until the mushrooms are tender.

Drain the mushrooms and reserve the vinegar.

Put the mushrooms into hot jars.

Add the sherry to the vinegar and pour over the mushrooms.

Seal and store for 1 month before using.

FIG AND LEMON PRESERVE

1 lb (450 g) figs
1 pint (600 ml/ 2½ cups) water
1½ lbs (675 g) sugar
Grated rind and juice of 2 lemons

Wash and dry the figs.

Remove the stalks.

Chop the figs and soak in the water for 24 hours.

Turn the figs and water into a large saucepan.

Add the sugar and bring to the boil.

Remove any scum as it forms.

Add the rind and the juice of the lemons to the boiling figs.

Boil rapidly until setting point is reached.

To test for setting point put a teaspoon of the mixture onto a cold saucer or plate. If the jam solidifies and wrinkles as it cools, then setting point has been reached.

Pour the mixture into warm, sterilised jars.

Leave to cool and cover and store when cold.

RHUBARB JAM

Makes about 4 lbs (1.75 kg)

3 lbs (1.5 kg) rhubarb
3 lbs (1.5 kg) sugar
1 lemon

Wash, trim and chop the rhubarb.

Place in a bowl with the sugar.

Squeeze the lemon and add the juice to the rhubarb.

Cover with a cloth and leave overnight.

Put the rhubarb and sugar into a preserving pan with a very little water.

Heat gently to dissolve the sugar.

Bring to the boil and cook until the rhubarb is tender, and setting point is reached.

To test for setting point put a teaspoon of the jam onto a cold saucer. If the jam solidifies and wrinkles as it cools, setting point has been reached.

Cool slightly and then pour into warm, sterilised jars.

Cover, cool and store.

PONTAC SAUCE

1½ lbs (675 g) ripe elderberries
¾ pint (450 ml/ 2 cups) vinegar
A small piece of root ginger
4 oz (100 g) shallots, chopped
A few cloves
A few peppercorns

Boil the vinegar.

Pour the vinegar over the elderberries.

Leave to stand for 24 hours in a warm place.

Strain the liquid and boil for 5 minutes with the root ginger, cloves, shallot and peppercorns.

Leave to cool, then bottle and seal when cold.

COUNTY SAUCE

This sauce is traditionally served with local pork pies.

1 lb (450 g) cooking apples
1 lb (450 g) tomatoes
1 lb (450 g) onions
Juice of 1 lemon
6 oz (175 g) sultanas
4 oz (100 g) sugar
2 pints (1.15 litres/ 5 cups) vinegar
1 oz (25 g) mixed spice
1 oz (25 g) cornflour
A large pinch of salt

Peel, core and chop the apples.

Skin and chop the tomatoes and onions finely.

Put the apple, tomatoes, onion, lemon juice, sultanas, sugar, vinegar, mixed spice and salt into a large saucepan.

Bring to the boil and simmer for 30 minutes or until the ingredients are soft.

Liquidize the mixture or rub it through a wire mesh sieve.

Return to the pan and bring to the boil.

Mix the cornflour with a little cold water and add to the sauce.

Cook until thick, stirring all the time.

Serve with pork pie or pour into jars, seal and store in a dry cool place.

STILTON SAUCE Makes 1½ pints (900ml/ 3¾ cups)

This sauce is traditionally served with grilled plaice.

2 oz (50 g) butter
2 oz (50 g) flour
1¼ pints (750ml/ 3 cups) milk
A pinch of salt
8 oz (225 g) Stilton cheese
¼ pint (150 ml/ ⅔ cup) double cream

Melt the butter over a low heat.

Add the flour and cook for a few minutes to make a roux.

Gradually add the milk stirring all the time.

Season with a pinch of salt.

Bring to the boil and simmer until thickened.

Crumble the Stilton cheese and add to the white sauce.

Stir over a low heat until the cheese has melted.

Add the double cream and heat gently but do not boil.

SALAD DRESSING

This recipe has been passed down through a Leicestershire family for nearly a hundred years.

1 heaped teaspoon flour
1 heaped teaspoon salt
1 heaped teaspoon sugar
1 heaped teaspoon made-up mustard
3 eggs
8 fl oz (250 ml/ 1 cup) milk
8 fl oz (250 ml/ 1 cup) water
8 fl oz (250 ml/ 1 cup) vinegar
A little pepper

Mix the flour, salt, sugar and mustard.

Add the eggs and beat well.

Add the milk and water and beat again.

Finally, add the vinegar and mix well.

Season with a little pepper.

Receipt for Toothache

Clean the teeth with a powder of seven eighths gunpowder and one eighth camphor.

To Keep Wet Out of Shoes

1 oz bees wax
½ oz burgundy pitch
1 pint linseed oil
2 oz spirit of turpentine

Mix the three first together over the fire in an Earthen Pot and then add the Turpentine.

Acknowledgements:

Grateful thanks are extended to the many people of Leicestershire who have contributed towards this collection of recipes, especially:

Mrs. Sybil Ross for Salad Dressing

Mrs. Susan Hall for Leicestershire Croustades

Leicestershire Record Office for Paradise Pudding poem (DE1214/4); and Receipt to Cure Toothache and To Keep Wet Out of Shoes (DE 258 CE/7) by kind permission of Mr S. Packe-Drury-Lowe.

THE COUNTRY RECIPE SERIES

Available now @ £1.95 each

Cambridgeshire
Cornwall
Cumberland & Westmorland
Devon
Dorset
Hampshire
Kent
Lancashire
Leicestershire
Norfolk
Oxfordshire
Somerset
Suffolk
Sussex
Warwickshire
Yorkshire

All these books are available at your local bookshop or newsagent, or can be ordered direct from the publisher. Just tick the titles you require and fill in the form below. Prices and availability subject to change without notice.

Ravette Books Limited, 3 Glenside Estate, Star Road, Partridge Green, Horsham, West Sussex RH13 8RA.

Please send a cheque or postal order, and allow the following for postage and packing. UK 25p for one book and 10p for each additional book ordered.

Name ....

Address ....

....

....